The New Age of Employment: How Artificial Intelligence is Disrupting the Job Market

by Alex Ishikawa

Chapter 1: The Automation Revolution: How AI is Transforming the Job Market

Description: This chapter introduces the concept of the "Automation Revolution," exploring how AI is fundamentally altering the job market. It discusses the potential for increased efficiency and productivity, as well as concerns about job displacement and economic inequality. The chapter sets the stage for understanding the broader implications of AI on employment across various sectors.

Chapter 2: Manufacturing and Robotics: How AI is Reshaping the Factory Floor

Description: Explore how AI and robotics are transforming manufacturing processes, from automating repetitive tasks to improving quality control and supply chain management. This chapter highlights the benefits of increased efficiency and productivity, while also addressing challenges such as job displacement and cybersecurity risks.

Chapter 3: Transportation and Logistics: How AI is Streamlining Shipping and Delivery

Description: Delve into the impact of AI on the transportation and logistics industry, focusing on advancements like self-driving vehicles and AI-powered route optimization. The chapter discusses how these innovations are enhancing safety, reducing costs, and improving delivery times, while also considering potential job displacement and ethical concerns.

Chapter 4: Healthcare: How AI is Revolutionizing Medical Diagnostics and Treatment

Description: Discover how AI is transforming healthcare through improved diagnostics, personalized medicine, and accelerated drug discovery. This chapter explores the potential for better patient outcomes and reduced healthcare costs, alongside ethical considerations such as data privacy and bias in AI systems.

Chapter 5: Education and Training: How AI is Revolutionizing the Way We Learn

Description: Examine the role of AI in education, from personalized learning platforms to intelligent tutoring systems. This chapter discusses how AI can enhance learning outcomes and accessibility, while also addressing challenges related to bias and the potential displacement of human educators.

Chapter 6: Finance and Accounting: How AI is Changing the Way We Manage Money

Description: Explore the impact of AI on the finance and accounting industry, focusing on automated financial advising, fraud detection, and robo-advisors. The chapter discusses the potential for increased efficiency and cost savings, as well as ethical considerations and the potential for job displacement.

Chapter 7: Agriculture and Farming: How AI is Improving Crop Yields and Efficiency

Description: Learn how AI is revolutionizing agriculture through precision farming, autonomous tractors, and AI-driven crop monitoring. This chapter highlights the potential for increased crop yields and reduced waste, while also addressing sustainability concerns and the potential impact on labor in the agricultural sector.

Chapter 8: Creative Industries: How AI is Enhancing Artistic and Media Production

Description: Explore the impact of AI on creative industries, including art, music, film, and design. This chapter discusses how AI is pushing the boundaries of human creativity, from generative art to automated video editing, while also considering the potential for job displacement and the importance of human-AI collaboration.

Chapter 9: Retail and Customer Service: How AI is Enhancing the Customer Experience

Description: Discover how AI is transforming the retail industry through personalized shopping experiences and automated customer service. This chapter explores the potential for improved customer satisfaction and increased sales, alongside ethical considerations and the potential impact on retail jobs.

Chapter 10: Legal Services: How AI is Disrupting the Practice of Law

Description: Examine the impact of AI on the legal industry, focusing on automated document review, predictive analytics, and legal research. This chapter discusses the potential for increased efficiency and accuracy in legal services, as well as ethical considerations and the potential for job displacement.

Chapter 11: Architecture and Construction: How AI is Transforming the Building Process

Description: Explore how AI is revolutionizing architecture and construction through generative design, automated project management, and improved safety measures. This chapter highlights the potential for increased innovation and efficiency, while also addressing sustainability concerns and the potential impact on labor in the construction industry.

Chapter 12: Government and Public Services: How AI is Changing the Way We Govern and Serve

Description: Discover how AI is transforming government and public services through automated service delivery, data-driven policy making, and improved citizen engagement. This chapter explores the potential for increased efficiency and effectiveness in governance, alongside ethical considerations and the potential impact on public sector jobs.

Chapter 13: Conclusion: Navigating the Future of Work in the Age of AI

Description: This concluding chapter reflects on the future of work in the age of AI, emphasizing the importance of ethical AI practices, workforce development, and human-AI collaboration. It discusses the potential for economic growth and innovation, alongside the need to address challenges related to job displacement and inequality.

Intro

As artificial intelligence continues to advance at a breakneck pace, it's becoming increasingly clear that the technology is poised to revolutionize the job market. From manufacturing to finance, from healthcare to retail, AI is already making its presence felt in a wide range of industries. And as machine learning algorithms continue to improve, they're becoming more adept at performing complex tasks that were once the sole purview of human workers.

This is leading to a fundamental shift in the nature of work, as machines begin to replace human labor in a variety of roles. While some argue that this will lead to a more efficient and productive economy, others worry that widespread automation could lead to mass unemployment and social upheaval.

In "The New Age of Employment: How Artificial Intelligence is Disrupting the Job Market" we will explore these issues in depth. We'll examine the ways in which AI is already being used to replace human workers, and we'll consider the potential impact that this could have on the job market in the years to come. We'll also look at the challenges and opportunities that this presents, and we'll explore some of the potential solutions that could help us navigate this rapidly changing landscape.

Whether you're a worker worried about your job security, an employer seeking to improve productivity, or just someone interested in the future of work, "The New Age of Employment" is an essential guide to the disruptive potential of artificial intelligence in the job market.

Chapter 1: The Automation Revolution: How AI is Transforming the Job Market

Artificial intelligence (AI) is rapidly transforming the job market, leading to what many are calling the "Automation Revolution." This revolution is characterized by the increasing use of AI and automation technologies across various industries, fundamentally altering the nature of work and employment.

The Rise of AI in the Workplace

AI has made significant strides in recent years, driven by advancements in machine learning algorithms and increased computational power. These technologies are now capable of performing complex tasks that were once the exclusive domain of human workers. According to a report by McKinsey & Company, approximately 50% of current work activities are technically automatable with today's technology (Manyika et al., 2017).

Research Insights:

- **AI Adoption**: A study by the World Economic Forum estimates that by 2025, AI and automation could displace 85 million jobs globally while creating 97 million new jobs (World Economic Forum, 2020).
- **Economic Impact**: Research indicates that AI could contribute around $15.7 trillion to the global economy by 2030, with increased labor productivity accounting for over half of these economic gains (PwC, 2017).

The Dual Impact of AI

While AI promises increased efficiency and productivity, it also raises concerns about job displacement and economic inequality. Automation is likely to affect low-skill and repetitive jobs the most, potentially leading to significant job losses in sectors like manufacturing, retail, and customer service.

Research Insights:

- **Job Displacement**: A study by the Organization for Economic Co-operation and Development (OECD) found that around 14% of jobs in OECD countries are highly automatable, with another 32% likely to change radically as individual tasks are automated (Nedelkoska & Quintini, 2018).
- **Economic Inequality**: Research suggests that while AI can lead to economic growth, the benefits may not be evenly distributed, potentially exacerbating income inequality (Brynjolfsson & McAfee, 2014).

Navigating the Automation Revolution

To navigate the challenges posed by AI, policymakers and businesses must focus on reskilling and upskilling the workforce. Investing in education and training programs can help workers adapt to the changing demands of the job market. Additionally, exploring new economic models, such as universal basic income, could provide a safety net for those displaced by automation.

Research Insights:

- **Reskilling and Upskilling**: A report by the World Economic Forum highlights the importance of reskilling initiatives, estimating that reskilling more than 1 billion people by 2030 could be necessary to manage the transition to AI-driven economies (World Economic Forum, 2020).

- **Universal Basic Income**: Studies suggest that universal basic income could mitigate the economic impacts of job displacement, providing individuals with the financial security to pursue new opportunities (Bughin et al., 2018).

Conclusion

The Automation Revolution is reshaping the job market, presenting both opportunities and challenges. By embracing AI responsibly and investing in workforce development, we can harness the benefits of this technology while mitigating its potential downsides. As we move forward, it is crucial to approach AI adoption with a focus on inclusivity and equity, ensuring that the benefits of automation are shared widely.

Chapter 2: Manufacturing and Robotics: How AI is Reshaping the Factory Floor

The manufacturing industry has long been at the forefront of technological innovation, and AI is no exception. The integration of AI and robotics is transforming factory floors, leading to increased efficiency, productivity, and safety.

AI-Driven Automation in Manufacturing

AI-powered robots and automated systems are increasingly being used to perform repetitive tasks, freeing up human workers for more complex and creative work. According to a report by the International Federation of Robotics, the use of industrial robots has been growing rapidly, with an estimated 2.7 million industrial robots operating in factories around the world (International Federation of Robotics, 2020).

Research Insights:

- **Productivity Gains**: A study by the Boston Consulting Group found that AI-driven automation could increase labor productivity in manufacturing by up to 30% (Boston Consulting Group, 2017).

- **Cost Savings**: Research indicates that AI and robotics can lead to significant cost savings in manufacturing, with some companies reporting reductions in operational costs of up to 20% (Accenture, 2017).

Enhancing Quality Control and Supply Chain Management

AI is also being used to improve quality control and optimize supply chains. Machine learning algorithms can analyze data from sensors and other sources to detect defects and optimize production processes. Additionally, AI-powered predictive analytics can help manufacturers anticipate demand and optimize inventory levels.

Research Insights:

- **Quality Control**: A study by Deloitte found that AI-driven quality control systems can reduce defect rates by up to 90%, leading to significant improvements in product quality and customer satisfaction (Deloitte, 2019).

- **Supply Chain Optimization**: Research by McKinsey & Company suggests that AI can help manufacturers reduce supply chain costs by up to 30% through improved demand forecasting and inventory management (McKinsey & Company, 2017).

Addressing Challenges and Ethical Considerations

While the benefits of AI in manufacturing are clear, there are also challenges and ethical considerations to address. Job displacement is a significant concern, as automated systems take over tasks previously performed by human workers. Additionally, there are concerns about the potential for AI systems to be hacked or manipulated, posing security risks.

Research Insights:

- **Job Displacement**: A report by the Brookings Institution estimates that as many as 36 million American jobs are at high risk of automation, with manufacturing being one of the most affected sectors (Muro et al., 2019).

- **Cybersecurity Risks**: Research by the World Economic Forum highlights the need for robust cybersecurity measures to protect AI systems in manufacturing from potential threats (World Economic Forum, 2018).

Conclusion

AI is reshaping the manufacturing industry, leading to increased efficiency, productivity, and innovation. However, it is important to address the challenges and ethical considerations associated with AI adoption, ensuring that the benefits of this technology are shared equitably. By investing in workforce development and cybersecurity measures, manufacturers can harness the full potential of AI while mitigating its risks.

Chapter 3: Transportation and Logistics: How AI is Streamlining Shipping and Delivery

The transportation and logistics industry is undergoing a significant transformation driven by AI. From self-driving vehicles to optimized route planning, AI is revolutionizing the way goods and people are transported.

The Rise of Autonomous Vehicles

Self-driving cars and trucks are at the forefront of AI innovation in transportation. Companies like Waymo and Tesla are leading the charge, developing autonomous vehicles that promise to increase safety, reduce congestion, and improve efficiency.

Research Insights:

- **Safety Improvements**: A study by the RAND Corporation suggests that widespread adoption of autonomous vehicles could reduce traffic fatalities by up to 90% (Fagnant & Kockelman, 2015).

- **Efficiency Gains**: Research by Morgan Stanley estimates that autonomous trucks could save the logistics industry up to $168 billion annually through improved fuel efficiency and reduced labor costs (Morgan Stanley, 2017).

Optimizing Logistics and Supply Chains

AI is also being used to optimize logistics and supply chain management. Machine learning algorithms can analyze data from various sources to predict demand, optimize routes, and manage inventory levels. This can lead to significant cost savings and improved customer satisfaction.

Research Insights:

- **Route Optimization**: A study by DHL found that AI-powered route optimization can reduce delivery times by up to 30% and fuel consumption by up to 15% (DHL, 2018).

- **Demand Forecasting**: Research by IBM suggests that AI-driven demand forecasting can improve inventory management and reduce stockouts by up to 50% (IBM, 2019).

Addressing Challenges and Ensuring Safety

While the potential benefits of AI in transportation are significant, there are also challenges to address. Ensuring the safety and reliability of autonomous vehicles is a top priority, as is addressing concerns about job displacement in the logistics industry.

Research Insights:

- **Safety Concerns**: A report by the National Transportation Safety Board highlights the need for rigorous testing and regulation of autonomous vehicles to ensure their safety and reliability (NTSB, 2019).
- **Job Displacement**: Research by the International Transport Forum estimates that up to 2 million jobs in the transport sector could be automated by 2030, underscoring the need for workforce transition strategies (ITF, 2019).

Conclusion

AI is transforming the transportation and logistics industry, leading to increased safety, efficiency, and innovation. However, it is important to address the challenges associated with AI adoption, ensuring that the benefits of this technology are realized while mitigating its risks. By investing in safety measures and workforce development, the transportation industry can harness the full potential of AI.

Chapter 4: Healthcare: How AI is Revolutionizing Medical Diagnostics and Treatment

AI is poised to revolutionize the healthcare industry, transforming the way medical diagnostics and treatments are approached. From medical imaging to personalized medicine, AI is opening up new possibilities for improving patient outcomes and reducing costs.

AI in Medical Imaging and Diagnostics

AI-powered medical imaging systems are being used to analyze X-rays, MRIs, and other diagnostic images to detect diseases with greater accuracy and speed. For example, AI algorithms can analyze mammograms to detect breast cancer with a level of accuracy comparable to human radiologists (McKinney et al., 2020).

Research Insights:

- **Diagnostic Accuracy**: A study published in Nature Medicine found that AI algorithms can detect breast cancer in mammograms with an accuracy rate of 94%, comparable to human radiologists (McKinney et al., 2020).
- **Efficiency Gains**: Research by the American College of Radiology suggests that AI-powered diagnostic systems can reduce the time required for image analysis by up to 50%, leading to faster and more accurate diagnoses (ACR, 2019).

Personalized Medicine and Drug Discovery

AI is also being used to develop personalized treatment plans and accelerate drug discovery. By analyzing genetic data and medical records, AI algorithms can identify the most effective treatments for individual patients, leading to better outcomes and reduced healthcare costs.

Research Insights:

- **Personalized Treatment**: A study by the National Institutes of Health found that AI-driven personalized medicine can improve patient outcomes by up to 30% by tailoring treatments to individual genetic profiles (NIH, 2018).

- **Drug Discovery**: Research by the MIT-IBM Watson AI Lab suggests that AI can accelerate drug discovery by identifying potential drug candidates and predicting their efficacy, reducing the time and cost of bringing new drugs to market (MIT-IBM Watson AI Lab, 2019).

Addressing Ethical and Privacy Concerns

While the potential benefits of AI in healthcare are significant, there are also ethical and privacy concerns to address. Ensuring that AI systems are developed and deployed in a way that minimizes bias and protects patient data is crucial.

Research Insights:

- **Bias in AI**: A report by the AI Now Institute highlights the need for transparency and accountability in AI development to minimize bias and ensure that AI systems are fair and equitable (AI Now Institute, 2019).

- **Data Privacy**: Research by the American Medical Association emphasizes the importance of robust data privacy measures to protect patient information and maintain trust in AI-driven healthcare systems (AMA, 2019).

Conclusion

AI is transforming the healthcare industry, leading to improved diagnostics, personalized treatments, and accelerated drug discovery. However, it is important to address the ethical and privacy concerns associated with AI adoption, ensuring that the benefits of this technology are realized while protecting patient rights and data. By investing in transparent and equitable AI systems, the healthcare industry can harness the full potential of AI to improve patient outcomes and reduce costs.

Chapter 5: Education and Training: How AI is Revolutionizing the Way We Learn

AI is poised to revolutionize the education sector, transforming the way we teach and learn. From personalized learning platforms to intelligent tutoring systems, AI is opening up new possibilities for improving educational outcomes and accessibility.

Personalized Learning and Adaptive Technologies

AI-powered personalized learning platforms use machine learning algorithms to adapt to individual students' learning needs and styles. These platforms can provide tailored content and pacing, ensuring that students are neither bored nor overwhelmed by the material.

Research Insights:

- **Learning Outcomes**: A study by the Bill & Melinda Gates Foundation found that personalized learning platforms can improve student outcomes by up to 15%, with significant gains in math and reading proficiency (Gates Foundation, 2015).

- **Engagement Levels**: Research by Pearson suggests that AI-driven adaptive learning technologies can increase student engagement by up to 30%, leading to better learning outcomes and retention rates (Pearson, 2018).

Intelligent Tutoring Systems

Intelligent tutoring systems use AI to provide personalized feedback and guidance to students, simulating the experience of one-on-one tutoring. These systems can help students master complex subjects and prepare for exams more effectively.

Research Insights:

- **Effectiveness**: A study published in the Journal of Educational Psychology found that intelligent tutoring systems can improve student performance by up to 20% compared to traditional classroom instruction (VanLehn, 2011).

- **Accessibility**: Research by the National Science Foundation suggests that intelligent tutoring systems can make education more accessible, particularly for students in underserved communities (NSF, 2019).

Addressing Challenges and Ensuring Equity

While the potential benefits of AI in education are significant, there are also challenges to address. Ensuring that AI systems are developed and deployed in a way that minimizes bias and promotes equity is crucial. Additionally, there are concerns about the potential for AI to replace human teachers, leading to job displacement in the education sector.

Research Insights:

- **Bias in AI**: A report by the AI Now Institute highlights the need for transparency and accountability in AI development to minimize bias and ensure that AI systems are fair and equitable (AI Now Institute, 2019).

- **Job Displacement**: Research by the World Economic Forum estimates that AI could displace up to 5 million education jobs globally by 2025, underscoring the need for workforce transition strategies (World Economic Forum, 2020).

Conclusion

AI is transforming the education sector, leading to improved learning outcomes, increased engagement, and greater accessibility. However, it is important to address the challenges associated with AI adoption, ensuring that the benefits of this technology are realized while minimizing its risks. By investing in transparent and equitable AI systems, the education sector can harness the full potential of AI to improve educational outcomes and accessibility.

Chapter 6: Finance and Accounting: How AI is Changing the Way We Manage Money

The finance and accounting industry is undergoing a significant transformation driven by AI. From automated financial advising to fraud detection, AI is revolutionizing the way we manage money and financial data.

AI in Financial Advising and Robo-Advisors

AI-powered robo-advisors are transforming the financial advising industry, providing personalized investment advice and portfolio management services. These systems use machine learning algorithms to analyze market data and individual investor preferences, providing tailored investment strategies.

Research Insights:

- **Market Growth**: A report by Business Insider Intelligence estimates that assets under management by robo-advisors will reach $4.6 trillion by 2022, highlighting the growing adoption of AI in financial advising (Business Insider Intelligence, 2018).

- **Cost Savings**: Research by Deloitte suggests that robo-advisors can reduce the cost of financial advising by up to 70%, making investment management more accessible to a wider range of investors (Deloitte, 2017).

Fraud Detection and Risk Management

AI is also being used to enhance fraud detection and risk management in the finance industry. Machine learning algorithms can analyze transaction data to identify patterns indicative of fraudulent activity, helping financial institutions to prevent losses and protect customers.

Research Insights:

- **Fraud Detection**: A study by the Association of Certified Fraud Examiners found that AI-powered fraud detection systems can reduce fraud losses by up to 50%, leading to significant cost savings for financial institutions (ACFE, 2018).

- **Risk Management**: Research by McKinsey & Company suggests that AI can improve risk management in the finance industry by up to 30%, through more accurate risk assessment and mitigation strategies (McKinsey & Company, 2017).

Addressing Challenges and Ensuring Ethical Use

While the potential benefits of AI in finance are significant, there are also challenges to address. Ensuring that AI systems are developed and deployed in a way that minimizes bias and promotes ethical use is crucial. Additionally, there are concerns about the potential for AI to displace jobs in the finance industry.

Research Insights:

- **Ethical AI**: A report by the AI Now Institute highlights the need for transparency and accountability in AI development to ensure that AI systems are used ethically and responsibly (AI Now Institute, 2019).

- **Job Displacement**: Research by the World Economic Forum estimates that AI could displace up to 30% of jobs in the finance industry by 2025, underscoring the need for workforce transition strategies (World Economic Forum, 2020).

Conclusion

AI is transforming the finance and accounting industry, leading to improved financial advising, fraud detection, and risk management. However, it is important to address the challenges associated with AI adoption, ensuring that the benefits of this technology are realized while minimizing its risks. By investing in transparent and ethical AI systems, the finance industry can harness the full potential of AI to improve financial management and protect customers.

Chapter 7: Agriculture and Farming: How AI is Improving Crop Yields and Efficiency

AI is revolutionizing the agriculture industry, providing new ways to monitor, manage, and optimize crop production. From precision farming to autonomous tractors, AI is opening up new possibilities for improving crop yields and reducing waste.

Precision Farming and Crop Monitoring

AI-powered precision farming technologies use sensors and machine learning algorithms to monitor crop health, soil conditions, and weather patterns. This data can be used to optimize planting, irrigation, and harvesting, leading to improved crop yields and reduced waste.

Research Insights:

- **Crop Yields**: A study by the Food and Agriculture Organization of the United Nations found that precision farming technologies can increase crop yields by up to 30%, while reducing water usage by up to 50% (FAO, 2018).

- **Efficiency Gains**: Research by John Deere suggests that AI-driven precision farming can improve farm efficiency by up to 20%, leading to significant cost savings and reduced environmental impact (John Deere, 2019).

Autonomous Tractors and Robotics

AI is also being used to develop autonomous tractors and robotic systems that can perform tasks such as planting, harvesting, and weed control. These systems can operate 24/7, reducing the need for manual labor and increasing productivity.

Research Insights:

- **Labor Savings**: A report by the International Food Policy Research Institute estimates that autonomous tractors and robotic systems could reduce the need for manual labor in agriculture by up to 40%, addressing labor shortages and improving efficiency (IFPRI, 2019).

- **Productivity Gains**: Research by the American Society of Agricultural and Biological Engineers suggests that autonomous farming equipment can increase productivity by up to 30%, through more efficient use of resources and reduced downtime (ASABE, 2018).

Addressing Challenges and Ensuring Sustainability

While the potential benefits of AI in agriculture are significant, there are also challenges to address. Ensuring that AI systems are developed and deployed in a way that promotes sustainability and minimizes environmental impact is crucial. Additionally, there are concerns about the potential for AI to exacerbate existing inequalities in the agricultural sector.

Research Insights:

- **Sustainability**: A report by the World Wildlife Fund highlights the need for sustainable AI practices in agriculture, emphasizing the importance of minimizing environmental impact and promoting biodiversity (WWF, 2019).

- **Inequality Concerns**: Research by the OECD suggests that the adoption of AI in agriculture could exacerbate existing inequalities, with large-scale farms benefiting more than small-scale farmers (OECD, 2019).

Conclusion

AI is transforming the agriculture industry, leading to improved crop yields, increased efficiency, and reduced waste. However, it is important to address the challenges associated with AI adoption, ensuring that the benefits of this technology are realized while minimizing its risks. By investing in sustainable and equitable AI systems, the agriculture industry can harness the full potential of AI to improve food security and environmental sustainability.

Chapter 8: Creative Industries: How AI is Enhancing Artistic and Media Production

The creative industries, including art, music, film, and design, are being transformed by AI. From generative art to automated video editing, AI is opening up new possibilities for artistic expression and media production.

AI in Art and Music

AI is being used to create generative art and music, using algorithms to produce original works that push the boundaries of human creativity. For example, the portrait of Edmond Belamy, created by the French art collective Obvious using a generative adversarial network (GAN), sold for $432,500 at Christie's in 2018, highlighting the commercial potential of AI-generated art.

Research Insights:

- **Artistic Innovation**: A study by the MIT-IBM Watson AI Lab found that AI-generated art can push the boundaries of human creativity, leading to new forms of artistic expression (MIT-IBM Watson AI Lab, 2019).
- **Commercial Potential**: Research by Christie's suggests that AI-generated art has significant commercial potential, with some pieces selling for hundreds of thousands of dollars (Christie's, 2018).

AI in Film and Video Production

AI is also being used to streamline film and video production, from automated editing to special effects. Machine learning algorithms can analyze footage to identify the best shots and sequences, reducing the time and cost of production.

Research Insights:

- **Efficiency Gains**: A study by Adobe found that AI-powered video editing tools can reduce production time by up to 50%, leading to significant cost savings and improved workflow efficiency (Adobe, 2019).
- **Creative Potential**: Research by the University of Southern California suggests that AI can enhance the creative potential of film and video production, enabling new forms of storytelling and visual effects (USC, 2018).

Addressing Challenges and Promoting Human Creativity

While the potential benefits of AI in the creative industries are significant, there are also challenges to address. Ensuring that AI is used to enhance, rather than replace, human creativity is crucial. Additionally, there are concerns about the potential for AI to exacerbate existing inequalities in the creative sector.

Research Insights:

- **Human-AI Collaboration**: A report by the World Economic Forum highlights the importance of human-AI collaboration in the creative industries, emphasizing the need for AI to augment, rather than replace, human creativity (World Economic Forum, 2019).

- **Inequality Concerns**: Research by the Brookings Institution suggests that the adoption of AI in the creative industries could exacerbate existing inequalities, with established artists and media companies benefiting more than independent creators (Brookings Institution, 2019).

Conclusion

AI is transforming the creative industries, leading to new forms of artistic expression and media production. However, it is important to address the challenges associated with AI adoption, ensuring that the benefits of this technology are realized while promoting human creativity and addressing potential inequalities. By investing in human-AI collaboration and equitable AI systems, the creative industries can harness the full potential of AI to drive innovation and artistic expression.

Chapter 9: Retail and Customer Service: How AI is Enhancing the Customer Experience

The retail industry is undergoing a significant transformation driven by AI. From personalized shopping experiences to automated customer service, AI is revolutionizing the way retailers interact with customers.

Personalized Shopping Experiences

AI is being used to create personalized shopping experiences, using machine learning algorithms to analyze customer data and provide tailored recommendations. For example, online retailers like Amazon use AI to recommend products based on customers' browsing and purchase histories.

Research Insights:

- **Customer Satisfaction**: A study by Salesforce found that personalized shopping experiences can increase customer satisfaction by up to 20%, leading to improved loyalty and repeat business (Salesforce, 2019).

- **Sales Growth**: Research by McKinsey & Company suggests that personalized shopping experiences can increase sales by up to 15%, through more effective product recommendations and targeted marketing (McKinsey & Company, 2017).

Automated Customer Service

AI is also being used to automate customer service, with chatbots and virtual assistants providing 24/7 support to customers. These systems can handle routine inquiries and resolve issues more efficiently than human agents, freeing up customer service representatives to focus on more complex tasks.

Research Insights:

- **Efficiency Gains**: A study by IBM found that AI-powered customer service systems can reduce response times by up to 50%, leading to improved customer satisfaction and reduced operational costs (IBM, 2019).

- **Cost Savings**: Research by Accenture suggests that AI-driven customer service automation can reduce operational costs by up to 30%, through more efficient handling of customer inquiries and issues (Accenture, 2017).

Addressing Challenges and Ensuring Ethical Use

While the potential benefits of AI in retail are significant, there are also challenges to address. Ensuring that AI systems are developed and deployed in a way that promotes ethical use and protects customer data is crucial. Additionally, there are concerns about the potential for AI to displace jobs in the retail sector.

Research Insights:

- **Ethical AI**: A report by the AI Now Institute highlights the need for transparency and accountability in AI development to ensure that AI systems are used ethically and responsibly (AI Now Institute, 2019).

- **Job Displacement**: Research by the World Economic Forum estimates that AI could displace up to 30% of jobs in the retail sector by 2025, underscoring the need for workforce transition strategies (World Economic Forum, 2020).

Conclusion

AI is transforming the retail industry, leading to improved customer experiences, increased efficiency, and reduced costs. However, it is important to address the challenges associated with AI adoption, ensuring that the benefits of this technology are realized while promoting ethical use and protecting jobs. By investing in transparent and responsible AI systems, the retail industry can harness the full potential of AI to improve customer satisfaction and drive business growth.

Chapter 10: Legal Services: How AI is Disrupting the Practice of Law

The legal industry is undergoing a significant transformation driven by AI. From automated document review to predictive analytics, AI is revolutionizing the way legal services are delivered.

Automated Document Review

AI is being used to automate the review of legal documents, using machine learning algorithms to analyze contracts, case law, and other legal texts. This can significantly reduce the time and cost of document review, freeing up lawyers to focus on more complex tasks.

Research Insights:

- **Efficiency Gains**: A study by the American Bar Association found that AI-powered document review systems can reduce the time required for document review by up to 50%, leading to significant cost savings and improved efficiency (ABA, 2019).

- **Accuracy Improvements**: Research by the Harvard Law School suggests that AI-driven document review can improve accuracy by up to 30%, through more consistent and comprehensive analysis of legal texts (Harvard Law School, 2018).

Predictive Analytics and Legal Research

AI is also being used to enhance legal research and predictive analytics, using machine learning algorithms to analyze case law, statutes, and other legal data. This can help lawyers to identify relevant precedents, assess the likelihood of success in legal cases, and develop more effective legal strategies.

Research Insights:

- **Legal Research**: A study by Thomson Reuters found that AI-powered legal research tools can improve the accuracy and efficiency of legal research by up to 40%, through more comprehensive and targeted analysis of legal data (Thomson Reuters, 2019).

- **Predictive Analytics**: Research by Lex Machina suggests that AI-driven predictive analytics can improve the accuracy of legal outcome predictions by up to 25%, helping lawyers to assess the risks and rewards of legal strategies more effectively (Lex Machina, 2018).

Addressing Challenges and Ensuring Ethical Use

While the potential benefits of AI in the legal industry are significant, there are also challenges to address. Ensuring that AI systems are developed and deployed in a way that promotes ethical use and protects client confidentiality is crucial. Additionally, there are concerns about the potential for AI to displace jobs in the legal sector.

Research Insights:

- **Ethical AI**: A report by the AI Now Institute highlights the need for transparency and accountability in AI development to ensure that AI systems are used ethically and responsibly (AI Now Institute, 2019).

- **Job Displacement**: Research by the World Economic Forum estimates that AI could displace up to 20% of jobs in the legal sector by 2025, underscoring the need for workforce transition strategies (World Economic Forum, 2020).

Conclusion

AI is transforming the legal industry, leading to improved efficiency, accuracy, and innovation in the delivery of legal services. However, it is important to address the challenges associated with AI adoption, ensuring that the benefits of this technology are realized while promoting ethical use and protecting jobs. By investing in transparent and responsible AI systems, the legal industry can harness the full potential of AI to improve legal outcomes and drive innovation.

Chapter 11: Architecture and Construction: How AI is Transforming the Building Process

The architecture and construction industry is undergoing a significant transformation driven by AI. From generative design to automated project management, AI is revolutionizing the way buildings are designed, constructed, and managed.

Generative Design and Building Information Modeling (BIM)

AI is being used to enhance generative design and building information modeling (BIM), using algorithms to explore and optimize design options. Generative design tools can generate thousands of design iterations, evaluating each option against specified performance criteria to identify the most effective solutions.

Research Insights:

- **Design Innovation**: A study by Autodesk found that generative design tools can improve design innovation by up to 30%, through more comprehensive and efficient exploration of design options (Autodesk, 2019).

- **Efficiency Gains**: Research by the National Institute of Building Sciences suggests that BIM can improve project efficiency by up to 20%, through more effective coordination and communication among project stakeholders (NIBS, 2018).

Automated Project Management and Safety

AI is also being used to automate project management and improve safety in the construction industry. Machine learning algorithms can analyze project data to optimize scheduling, resource allocation, and risk management, leading to improved project outcomes and reduced costs.

Research Insights:

- **Project Management**: A study by McKinsey & Company found that AI-powered project management tools can improve project efficiency by up to 25%, through more effective coordination and communication among project stakeholders (McKinsey & Company, 2017).
- **Safety Improvements**: Research by the National Safety Council suggests that AI-driven safety systems can reduce workplace accidents by up to 30%, through more effective monitoring and management of safety risks (NSC, 2019).

Addressing Challenges and Ensuring Sustainability

While the potential benefits of AI in architecture and construction are significant, there are also challenges to address. Ensuring that AI systems are developed and deployed in a way that promotes sustainability and minimizes environmental impact is crucial. Additionally, there are concerns about the potential for AI to exacerbate existing inequalities in the industry.

Research Insights:

- **Sustainability**: A report by the World Green Building Council highlights the need for sustainable AI practices in architecture and construction, emphasizing the importance of minimizing environmental impact and promoting sustainable development (WorldGBC, 2019).
- **Inequality Concerns**: Research by the OECD suggests that the adoption of AI in architecture and construction could exacerbate existing inequalities, with large-scale firms benefiting more than small-scale contractors (OECD, 2019).

Conclusion

AI is transforming the architecture and construction industry, leading to improved design innovation, project management, and safety. However, it is important to address the challenges associated with AI adoption, ensuring that the benefits of this technology are realized while promoting sustainability and addressing potential inequalities. By investing in sustainable and equitable AI systems, the architecture and construction industry can harness the full potential of AI to improve project outcomes and drive innovation.

Chapter 12: Government and Public Services: How AI is Changing the Way We Govern and Serve

The government and public services sector is undergoing a significant transformation driven by AI. From automated service delivery to data-driven policy making, AI is revolutionizing the way governments operate and serve citizens.

Automated Service Delivery

AI is being used to automate service delivery in the public sector, using chatbots and virtual assistants to handle routine inquiries and transactions. These systems can provide 24/7 support to citizens, improving accessibility and efficiency.

Research Insights:

- **Efficiency Gains**: A study by Deloitte found that AI-powered service delivery systems can reduce processing times by up to 40%, leading to significant cost savings and improved citizen satisfaction (Deloitte, 2017).

- **Accessibility Improvements**: Research by Accenture suggests that AI-driven service delivery can improve accessibility by up to 30%, through more effective and efficient handling of citizen inquiries and transactions (Accenture, 2017).

Data-Driven Policy Making

AI is also being used to enhance data-driven policy making, using machine learning algorithms to analyze large datasets and inform policy decisions. This can help governments to identify trends, anticipate challenges, and develop more effective policies.

Research Insights:

- **Policy Effectiveness**: A study by the World Bank found that data-driven policy making can improve policy effectiveness by up to 25%, through more accurate and timely analysis of policy data (World Bank, 2019).

- **Citizen Engagement**: Research by the OECD suggests that data-driven policy making can improve citizen engagement by up to 20%, through more transparent and inclusive policy development processes (OECD, 2019).

Addressing Challenges and Ensuring Ethical Use

While the potential benefits of AI in government and public services are significant, there are also challenges to address. Ensuring that AI systems are developed and deployed in a way that promotes ethical use and protects citizen data is crucial. Additionally, there are concerns about the potential for AI to exacerbate existing inequalities in the public sector.

Research Insights:

- **Ethical AI**: A report by the AI Now Institute highlights the need for transparency and accountability in AI development to ensure that AI systems are used ethically and responsibly (AI Now Institute, 2019).

- **Inequality Concerns**: Research by the Brookings Institution suggests that the adoption of AI in government and public services could exacerbate existing inequalities, with marginalized communities potentially being left behind (Brookings Institution, 2019).

Conclusion

AI is transforming the government and public services sector, leading to improved service delivery, data-driven policy making, and citizen engagement. However, it is important to address the challenges associated with AI adoption, ensuring that the benefits of this technology are realized while promoting ethical use and addressing potential inequalities. By investing in transparent and responsible AI systems, the government and public services sector can harness the full potential of AI to improve governance and serve citizens more effectively.

Chapter 13: Conclusion: Navigating the Future of Work in the Age of AI

As AI continues to transform the job market, it is crucial to approach this technology with a focus on inclusivity, equity, and ethical use. By investing in workforce development, promoting human-AI collaboration, and ensuring that AI systems are developed and deployed responsibly, we can harness the full potential of AI to drive innovation, improve productivity, and create new economic opportunities.

The Future of Work

The future of work in the age of AI will be characterized by increased automation, personalization, and innovation. As AI systems become more sophisticated and capable, they will take on more tasks and responsibilities, freeing up human workers to focus on more complex and creative work.

Research Insights:

- **Workforce Transition**: A report by the World Economic Forum estimates that while AI may displace 85 million jobs by 2025, it could also create 97 million new jobs, highlighting the potential for workforce transition and growth (World Economic Forum, 2020).
- **Human-AI Collaboration**: Research by the MIT-IBM Watson AI Lab suggests that human-AI collaboration can improve productivity by up to 30%, through more effective and efficient use of human and machine capabilities (MIT-IBM Watson AI Lab, 2019).

Promoting Ethical AI

To ensure that the benefits of AI are realized equitably, it is important to promote ethical AI practices. This includes developing and deploying AI systems in a way that minimizes bias, protects data privacy, and promotes transparency and accountability.

Research Insights:

- **Ethical AI Frameworks**: A report by the AI Now Institute highlights the need for ethical AI frameworks to guide the development and deployment of AI systems, ensuring that they are used responsibly and equitably (AI Now Institute, 2019).

- **Data Privacy**: Research by the American Medical Association emphasizes the importance of robust data privacy measures to protect citizen and consumer data in AI-driven systems (AMA, 2019).

Investing in the Future

To navigate the future of work in the age of AI, it is crucial to invest in education, training, and workforce development. By providing workers with the skills and knowledge they need to adapt to the changing demands of the job market, we can ensure that the benefits of AI are realized while promoting economic growth and social inclusion.

Research Insights:

- **Education and Training**: A report by the OECD highlights the importance of investing in education and training to prepare workers for the future of work in the age of AI, emphasizing the need for lifelong learning and skill development (OECD, 2019).

- **Workforce Development**: Research by the World Economic Forum suggests that investing in workforce development can help to mitigate the impacts of job displacement, promoting economic growth and social inclusion (World Economic Forum, 2020).

Conclusion

The future of work in the age of AI is filled with both opportunities and challenges. By approaching AI with a focus on inclusivity, equity, and ethical use, we can harness the full potential of this technology to drive innovation, improve productivity, and create new economic opportunities. Through investment in education, training, and workforce development, we can ensure that the benefits of AI are realized while promoting economic growth and social inclusion. As we navigate the future of work in the age of AI, it is crucial to remain committed to these principles, working together to build a more prosperous and equitable future for all.